IN THE FLESH

IN THE FLESH

Poems

Adam O'Riordan

W. W. NORTON & COMPANY
Independent Publishers Since 1923
NEW YORK • LONDON

For information about permission to reproduce selections from this book,
write to Permissions, W. W. Norton & Company, Inc.,
500 Fifth Avenue, New York, NY 10110

For information about special discounts for bulk purchases, please contact
W. W. Norton Special Sales at specialsales@wwnorton.com or 800-233-4830

Manufacturing by RRD Westford
Production manager: Louise Mattarelliano

Library of Congress Cataloging-in-Publication Data

O'Riordan, Adam, 1982–
[Poems. Selections]
In the flesh / Adam O'Riordan. — First American edition.
pages ; cm
ISBN 978-0-393-34572-8 (softcover)
I. Title.
PR6065.R684A6 2015
821'.914—dc23

2015028386

W. W. Norton & Company, Inc.
500 Fifth Avenue, New York, N.Y. 10110
www.wwnorton.com

W. W. Norton & Company Ltd.
Castle House, 75/76 Wells Street, London W1T 3QT

ACKNOWLEDGMENTS

Acknowledgments are due to the editors of the following publications: *Agenda, Cumberland News, Guardian.co.uk, Harper's Bazaar, The Ladder, Limelight, The Madison Review, Magma, Oxford Magazine, Oxford Poetry, Poetry Review, The Turner Society Newsletter, Vice Magazine, The Wolf.*

Versions of some of these poems appeared in *Bedford Square* (John Murray), *Queen of the Cotton Cities* (Tall Lighthouse), *Voice Recognition: 21 Poets for the 21st Century* (Bloodaxe), *A Poet's Guide to Britain* (Penguin) and *Penguin's Poems for Love* (Penguin). The sequence *Home* first appeared in a limited edition pamphlet from The Wordsworth Trust.

The writing of these poems has been greatly assisted by an Arts Council England Writers' Award, an Eric Gregory Award from The Society of Authors and a year in residence at The Wordsworth Trust.

Special thanks to Clara Farmer and Parisa Ebrahimi for their support and encouragement with the manuscript. And to Sarah Chalfant at the Wylie Agency and Jill Bialosky at W. W. Norton & Company for giving these poems a life in the U.S.A.

CONTENTS

IN THE FLESH

MANCHESTER

Queen of the cotton cities,
nightly I piece you back into existence:

the frayed bridal train your chimneys lay
and the warped applause-track of Victorian rain.

You're the blackened lung whose depths I plumb,
the million windows and the smoke-occluded sun.

A girl steps from a door and her cotton-flecked shawl
is the first snow on a turf-plot back in Mayo.

You're the globing of the world, a litany of cities
cast and re-made in your image: *Osaka, Orizaba, Gabrovo.*

Your warehouses bloated by curious needs:
butter, shellfish, clog blocks, bleach.

Your urchins, little merchants, hawking Lucifers and besoms
to set a small flame guttering in a wet-brick basement:

in straw and wood shavings, a mother's lullabies
bear their freight of love and typhus.

In the small hours I remake you and remake you,
until you grow faint as a footfall on a fever ward

and I wake from my imagination's gas-lit parlour.
Whatever I seek to have or hold or harbour

is pure curio – a wreath of feathers, seashells
or human hair: a taxidermist's diorama.

1

VANISHING POINTS

I *Beach Huts, Milford, 1930*

These are the high-tide mark in this family's life;
    they huddle together, mugging for the Box-Brownie,
basking in the salt-air and sun between two wars,
    the lacuna of a first summer down from school:
a barefoot father in tie and starched collar,
    a mother's equine calm, as two boys shy like foals
around her. One will wake each night in later life
    to a friend's screams from inside a burning tank.
One in middle-age, at his mother's bedside, will wildly shake
    a bell for nurse, then drive in silence to collect the priest.
Today as you pose before the row of huts,
    in a silence folded between the wave and the wash,
I think of our life together becoming utterly lost,
    and lift this camera like a bible for an oath.

II *A Wedding Letter, Edinburgh, 1906*

Long after the site of any headstone was forgotten
    you live on in the letter my ancestor, the customs-man,
gave to his daughter the night of her wedding.
    Knitted in a chain mail script, your identity clings
like a broken web to a windowsill, as he recalls
    how, as a boy at your fireside, a *shanachie*
traced their family back to the garden of Eden.
    How you procured medicines for childhood diseases,
at wakes would carry your hospitality to extravagance,
    and never spoke English with any satisfaction.
Big-hearted drunk, shy of my mother tongue:
    I roll your word for liquor, *usquebaugh,* around my mouth.
You are distilled before you disappear forever
    like the raised glass, the sunlight on one last golden measure.

III *A Trade Union College, Dunfermline, 1983*

Familiar from the outset but unplaceable.
    Your rusted car reeled down the avenue
to waiting shop-stewards bussed in from Glasgow.
    You were distracted all morning before the flipchart
and paced like an artist irked by his sitter.
    Something rubbing at the edge of your consciousness:
a vision of forceps in a bowl of cooling water,
    cotton swabs fallen like split fruit to the floor,
the clocks in the house all hushed, then a midwife's laughter
    floats up like a paper rose; you are parked on the gravel
outside, your mother lifts you by the elbows to point out
    the room where she first came into this world.
Ashen-faced at the bar, the foreman stands you another
round:
    I seen that wreck of yours outside, son, you've no spot like this now.

NGC3949

A galaxy in Ursa Major whose formation mirrors, almost exactly,
that of our own.

Back from the perforated dark and growing distance,
Hubble's milky image brings us to ourselves.

The echo pitched up from the moss-wet well:
a lover's shape, that indelible stain on the iris.

(Years down the line, you swear blind
the cut and sway of a dark form is her.

Neon dazzles the rain-slicked street
as you wave away the cab and push

back down through the crowd into the bar,
pilot charting the wrong star by candlelight,

leagues off course; the face, of course, is another's.)
In this spiral galaxy the arms embrace the core.

Not her – or your idea of her – and never will be.
It doesn't matter how beautiful your guess is.

GOOOOGLE

A prayer then
for the men who sit,
pale as geishas,
by the glow of obsolete
computers.

Whose nights are never-
ending searches:
the busy crickets
of their fingers
stoking engines

with maiden names
and zip codes
of ex-lovers.
God of false trails
and disappearing acts,

deliver us
from the namesake:
Homecoming Queen,
Quaker settler,
tenured academic,

these indices of others.
It's getting light.
See how the dawn
seems to bleed
from Venus.

THE WHETSTONE

Summers flung us from our orbit
but to step into the weather of that room,
all stripped wood and sauna smell,
was to dispel any thoughts of home.

Here, skeins of rope loomed
like a hangman's apparatus,
gaudy knots transformed themselves
into the head of the Medusa.

His scythe rusting in the corner,
precise as a prosthetic limb.
The little window offering
a landscape lunar in its unfamiliarity.

Here he assembled objects of another life,
wading waist-deep into fields at first light,
body rolling against a wave of corn,
remote and lonely as an astronaut.

Alone in that loft we'd fire the whetstone,
rushing to find a rusted blade or bolt to touch
against the spinning device, gently as a field-nurse
might stoop to sanitize a wound.

Unquenchable at our font of shallow-fire
and cooling sparks but fearful
of how blindly it would part flesh,
bloody a foreknuckle, make a relic of a finger bone.

My father crept through the same door,
worked a skinny fist at this same wheel.
He knew, as we knew then, that once begun,
to let up would surely slip

the moorings of the battered canvas sun,
dim the wattage of the harvest moon,
snuff each star in the encroaching dark,
that only in such ways might we leave our mark.

THE MOTH

landed between *paper tiger* and *paperweight*
on the open dictionary, just short of *papillon.*
A natural under the spotlight,
drawn in from the night's hot lung
towards its sixty watts of promise.
Perfect, the disciplined pulse of its wings:
two coffee-stained teeth and all the grace

of your grandmother in her wedding dress.
This you will know from the message I left.
But I didn't mention the *tipulidae*, the *chironomidae*,
that I had to kill the lights and I'm sitting
on a bed too small to contain your absence,
listening to something the size of a small bird
ricocheting off the walls, clicking like a stuck tape.

THE CORPSE GARDEN

Knoxville, Tennessee

Winter nights in my hut, by the roar of the freeway,
I listen to the game in snatches on the transistor

then pull on my hat and pace the perimeter.
These gates could hold a car-lot or a workshop

or a proscenium arch. It's a little part of each:
this patch of campus cordoned-off behind

a padlock the size of a human heart.
Pity the freshman who vaults them to find nothing

but a badly tended garden: water butts, mulch bins,
battered tarpaulins where exposed toes might

belong to children camping under starlight.
I stay with the dead through their putrefaction,

mapping the body's catastrophic geography.
Nursemaids to insects, their skin laced with eggs

like strings of pearls sewn in a gown.
Fire ants clean the flesh then bow to blow-flies,

so we learn to fix the time since a body's demise
for when dental records or driving licences let us down

or when a corpse has lain so long overlooked
as now out there in some canyon the wind wheels

around a pile of bones and a scrap of party dress.
Apprenticed to their decay, I lift a plastic lid,

look down on a soup of bones, muscle lifting away.
Others in rows, skin like scrolls in an abandoned library,

moonlight on their blistered lips as if their last words
burned to speak but what they say is always lost.

This is when the wind gets up; the sportscaster
announces overtime, the crowd comes to life;

I pull up my collar and head inside,
rattling the fence at the foxes who gather

wondering why we have prepared such a feast,
but will not invite them to come-on-in and eat.

SCAR TISSUE

When my hand finds your arm in the dark,
more often than not it's that glossy cicatrice
where one drunk winter you fell asleep
against the dull heat of a cast-iron radiator.
My fingers map the known world of its contour:
your lonely archipelago. The keloid scar grows
and grows until it will not let either of us go.
Greek *eschara*, your 'place of fire', defines you:
that intimacy with the impulses that drew
you to burn for a love you could not name,
and walking home in the drizzling rain
the man, inarticulate with rage, who flicks
a flame towards the shadow of the Cutty Sark.

BLOSSOM

This knuckle
            of petals
twisted from the branch,
held like a match
to your sleeping face,

so the next breath you take
            will draw you
from a private dark,
slow the carousel
of blood-bright shapes,

as ammonium carbonate
            or a burning feather
might revive a castaway:
naked, salt-bitten, sun-wrecked,
the wind at her heart.

THE EDGES OF LOVE

I *A College Window, Cambridge*

The conference took you to Cambridge.
    An hour to kill you prowled your allotted room,
spare, perfunctory, like a cat dropped at a cattery,
    letting your tired mind tick over aimlessly;
imagining your mother's bicycle as she freewheeled
    home down a nearby lane, head full of algebra,
how you might have spent your own years here.
    Then you see a figure crossing the field by your window;
from two decades away you recognize her, a palpitation
    shoots from heart to scrotum. You want to call her name.
The sun is setting. Back home in a bright room
    your children are being kissed and tucked into their sheets.
After a pause that lasts your adult life, you turn from her
    draw the curtain, dim the lamp, walk down to supper.

II *A Department Store Escalator, Paris*

The screaming baby woke you three nights in a row
    like a fire engine wailing its alarm
through the 13th arrondissement. So the next day
    you carry your babe in arms like the Romany woman
that tugged at your mac for a handful of francs.
    Your specs are smudged, the baby like a sack of flour
as you ride the department store escalator, a finger
    resting against its teething gums, rising above
the riot of scent. A stranger descends. Your gazes hold
    and a lifetime unfolds: waking naked in the half-light,
smoothing her dark mane, your unborn children's names,
    your bones laid on hers in the grave,
at which she disappears again. In the café your wife asks
    why you're so distracted. *Nothing*, you tell her, *it's nothing.*

DRESSING

Up early, the sun barely able to throw
a shadow through the loose casement
that rattled like a freight-car far into our sleep.

You turn on the lamp and in its glow begin:
Cashmere, Touche Éclat, Kohl, Clinique,
a rose petal tincture dabbed onto your cheeks.

The blinds half-lowered like eyelids
as if this room strained to reconstruct you
between the white walls of its memory.

As you eclipse your winter skin,
the waking world begins to draw you back
and dulls what claims I thought I had.

Dressed you leave. Holding the sun's gaze,
the house articulates you perfectly.

TRAWLING

The tiniest fracture could stop the satellite,
travelling in silence through the vacuum's
detritus, that warns of a cloud bank sixty
leagues out from a small republic

struggling with insurgency and pandemic.
The pilot announces they'll fly above it.
A grandmother presses her cold nose
to the porthole but cannot make out

the rocking horse of the trawler below;
the smell of spilt diesel, fish guts,
blood and brine, gravity in flux;
a coffee cup slides along the galley,

its thick dregs are J.M.W. Turner's
Snowstorm: Steamboat off a Harbour's Mouth.

MANUEL URIBE GARZA

who, at his heaviest, weighed 1,320 lb

The landslide of his swollen limbs
is worn in patches to rhino-skin,
this grainy footage captures him
weeping in broken English for help,
it's as if he has kidnapped himself.
The face of a handsome mariachi,
a walrus on a deserted beach
as the orderly tugs at his hot sheets.

When he shed half his weight,
they paraded him through San Nicolas
de los Garza on a flatbed truck
like a plaster saint, a returning king
or something the fishermen brought in
but could not, for the life of them, name.

MY FATHER IN THE GARDEN

A shy man but
a showman in
this his quarter
acre of hemp seed
and crab apple,
of performing
arts the slowest.

HOME

'presently we saw a raven very high above us . . . it called again
& again as it flew onwards, & the mountains gave back the sound
. . . We heard both the call of the bird & the echoe after we could
see him no longer.'
                    Dorothy Wordsworth's Journal, July 1800

Candle Moulds

Pig fat, goose fat, tallow, they lie like corpses
in their narrow cots, fingers in a drowned
girl's glove, or barrels full of pistol shot.
Their smut and smoke will paint the parlour black
but tonight they let her sew a little longer
let him pace his mind's shoreline,
each thought a wave that breaks against
the shingle of type on the printed page
as night spills its ink across the vale
and the stars are wax spots on a hearthstone.
Tomorrow will bring rain, a hike in taxes,
rumours from the camps of defeated armies.
But tonight their flames speak of a frugal industry,
what light they made, what light there might yet be.

Silver Lake

'This life isn't all hookers-and-blow, you know'
but even so one day a month you'd ease the car off
the boulevard, your u-turn describing a long slow arc,
forgetting the pretence of work, the litter of scripts
on your passenger seat. Driving south
against the rush hour, the commute, as a salmon
might make its way, by force of will, upstream.
And so you headed out towards Tijuana.
I remember you saying you could order from a menu.
How the oiled girls lined up to meet-n-greet you.
But I could not tell you which part of yourself
you handed over as your Buick crawled across the border.
Or which part of yourself you left forever
with Tanya, Tracy-Mae, Encarnación or Estella.

A Double Wash Stand

Before the age condemned such joint ablutions
you dip your hands in the tepid water
as the geese come in low across the lake
landing on their shadows, becoming their wake,
breaking apart the imago they seemed to chase.
So you break this tension, shattering your own reflections.
There is a complicity in getting clean together
who knows what distances you travelled in your sleep,
drawn back towards one another,
and the secrets that those distances will keep.
Each movement fluid and practised in the winter air,
you revel in this intimate act, not quite each other's double.
You mime the mannerisms of other lives
like brother and sister; I mean, man and wife.

Dun Laoghaire

Each week at the drawing school you make ends meet.
So for the next hour you will stand, stripped,
turning like a hare on a spit, as they have you
from every angle: their charcoal thumbed
and smudged and rendered not-quite-right.
There are other records of this time,
curling in meter-cupboards or crumbling
under dust sheets in second-best guest rooms
but none record you blowing in your fist
to elongate the frail gourd of your cock and balls,
the sweep of the second hand, as you stand
like a sinner at the centre of a circle formed for prayer.
Behind the screen, the brown and mauves of autumn clothes
still warm, like a pile of leaves in which the fire won't hold.

An Apron Pocket

The sunlight on her bonnet makes her face
a lamp that throws its gaze far into the future.
What is this urge that sends her tramping
miles from home? Her apron pocket bleeding
seed down that dress's roughly sewn seam.
Her hands hinge open, the palm full of dust
blown on the air like the birth of a star.
But next year they are the heart-shaped leaves
of celandine: cure for haemorrhoids and scurvy,
that grassy-leaved, rabbit-toothed, white flower
identified for her new neighbours as stichwort,
and the bright heads conspicuously out of place,
their occurrence this far from home foxing botanists
and other off-comers for years into the future.

Sandy Hook

The telegram from Mr Humphrey Barton
arrived the day of your youngest son's wedding.
You took the night train to Lymington, sailed
together into the Atlantic on the cusp of springtime.
Navigating like a monk at his illuminations,
blown off course, your thin sleep broken
by a persistent dream: a junior police officer
sent to the edge of empire; a tubercular thief;
a battered body tethered to a bamboo tree.
Then your sobbing fills the small boat's hull.
A flotilla met you at the lip of the harbour;
like a confessor, you whispered to the newscaster
at the Public Radio station about the birds
that followed you all the way across the ocean.

A Hearth Fire

Dark heart nested in the bowels of the house.
It burned unbroken for a hundred years.
Its one idea was permanence.
A slow but restless beast they all obeyed,
duly fed a glut of twigs and sticks and coal
as it ate away the soft hours of their lives,
lodged a dull ache in the back of their minds.
Their days, it seemed at times, were built
around the protestations of its glowing mouth,
that relentlessly unsatiated appetite,
its sly moods and grades of heat and light.
At midnight, waking to a gale outside, the fear
that a soot fall or change in weather
might sever this link with their past for ever.

Heidelberg

You're just sixteen and hitching across Europe
both bleary-eyed as the Mercedes glides up,
the block of hash like a moon rock in your pocket.
You throw your bags in the back, one of you dozes off.
The porcine driver practises his few phrases of English
and pretty soon you know exactly what he wants,
his prick a pink tongue lapping from his suit pants.
Like a calf trapped in the back of an abattoir van,
that sickness as the world outside slows to a stop.
Now you're running through the long grass, breathless,
laughter, like lava, burning up and out of your throats,
collapsing together a mile from the autobahn.
And now your friend is forty years old, and you wake
in mortgaged houses, much more to protect than each other.

A Bedstead

Sleeping upright to fend off the vapours,
the bed is a barouche that delivers you
through acres of night to daylight.
The crow's wing of its covered top to capture
the snake-flies, lacewings, hawkmoths,
that would fall like black thoughts
around your shoulders. Your trunk waits,
the lettering buckles at the far end where
you misjudged the length of your name.
A lifetime away, a lost love grieves; your daughter
grows a little older and more unknown.
But for now your carriage carries you no further
than dawn, where you wake to that same mist-
stilled horizon, that same damp-walled room.

Teatralnaya

Thirty years late you make it there, on business,
a clenched fist raised under Marx's granite face.
Below the statue a flash captures you mid-blink
remembering how you found the Manifesto
one lonely winter at a London crammer. Earlier
you burned $90 on burgers and beers in the Marriott diner
on expenses with colleagues fresh in from Idaho.
For you a career was always more a retirement.
Though, as you passed the red sauce, I doubt you
let them know the weather outside brought to mind
the day you drove a trunk full of pickaxe handles
across the Pennines to the striking miners
or the pistols still buried in the Portuguese foothills
by Mauricio who, in the winter of '73, taught you to fire them.

A Dance in the Kitchen

Late autumn, mothers gather in the kitchen
by pipe smoke and the moan of a horse-hair bow
on the hollow body of a fiddle. Drawn down
from his revisions he looks in as the dance's tattoo
grows to the sound of sleet on a slate roof,
then the beat of hooves across an open field
a blurring as somewhere in the fabric of these walls
the house recalls a former life: repository of gossip
and grief, the drunken seat of weary, heavy-handed
seductions, serving girls and wounded veterans.
Outside the mountains huddle like beggars at a brazier,
the town drunk puzzles up at the blind-eye of the moon,
the constellations a great broken mirror
that might tell us our fates could we piece it together.

Painted Eggs

Behind the house, altogether unseen,
their tiny ghosts call out from the trees.

THE LEVERETS

That first winter, cooing around your pink face
at the cradle, the purr of the wood-burner
flicking its long tail out into the night sky.
I was sent to the car for nappies and formula
but froze when I saw it laid on the porch:
the heavens condensed in its brown eye,
a frail bag of fur spilt a fine rope of gut
still warm to the touch as I went to move it.
Clawed from its nest into the cold world
sudden and bright and in a moment over.
This feline votive, carried across neighbours'
fields with that safe-breaker's swagger.
Then nothing, for years, until the birth of your sister.

CHEAT

As in the beach scene framed on this postcard,
where a jovial uncle is packed into sand
until even his head disappears below ground.
Just so, Ovid tells how unchaste Vestal Virgins
were shovelled under, quite alive but drowsy,
no longer afraid of the dark or the weight
of the dirt that would drown them.

In this dingy pub, cinders in a grate dust over.
I dab the tip of my nose for your odour,
remembering how, like a pontiff wet with balm
when anointing, I sunk with the fluke of your hips,
our movements incessant as a distaff and spindle.
Then, with him away and your place empty,
how we changed, stepped up our game and conjured:

two mongrel dogs locked and hot with instinct,
became a horse the rider moves in time with.
Then our spent bodies: eels fetched up in a bucket.
Night reclaims the light, a bell chimes,
my glass is drained; through the window pane
the interior steadies itself on the street.
I watch the stream of passers-by walk through me.

ON FIXING A BLOODY MARY

First the ice, then Stoli-O,
tomato juice, a splash of Tabasco;

this inexact equation of fruit and grain
balanced with a twist of pepper

like the aerial view of the woods
you ran through that humid summer

or closer, the coarse hair of your pubis,
tapering to a delicate red.

A crucible of molten lead,
the clench of blood in a beating heart.

Now part your lips and taste
yourself in this first sip –

the head of a battery, old pennies,
citrus, cumin, fermented honey.

OYSTERS

Back from the fish market's opening exchanges,
we spill our cache across the kitchen table.

First we discard the dead, those that will not give
or acquiesce, hoarding pearls in hoods of flesh.

Knuckles flecked with ribbons of red, we attempt
to shuck those left, unversed in this undressing

not knowing the balance of force and finessing.
Until you twist a blunt blade and the adductor severs

and light moves in the darkened chamber.
Naked on its bed of bone, you offer it: vulviform, raw,
exposed.

I swallow an ocean into silence and peristalsis,
it hangs like a four-letter word in my gullet.

MAREOTIS

A tongue of land
splits you, aching,
        from the ocean.
This lake reduced
to a dream of the sea.
        You long to feel
tides drag you free,
the salt's relentless
intimacy.

PORTRAIT OF A COPPER BEECH

A handsome man's laughter
as he dresses
for the cocktail hour.

★

In the breeze
the bellied sail
on a schooner.

★

Rush hour,
each leaf loose-change
spilled on the street.

★

In a cage of air
the bones
of a traitor.

PORTRAIT OF A BARN OWL

Ghost Owl Church Owl Rat Owl Stone Owl
you broke from the bough and no name could contain you.

The farmer's darling, you occur on every continent,
your appetite more economical than poison.

REVENANTS

Tonight, as the kettle cools on the hob,
tour groups fold away their maps,
matching anoraks, stow walking poles,
forsake these lanes for the A roads,

their tyres hiss away like static on a radio,
there's a sense of something coming back.
Outside the kitchen window the coffin path
emerges beneath the tourist track,

where dead generations were led
from godless towns to consecrated ground.
I picture them on a summer night struggling
with the big sling as if the body wrapped

within was simply dozing in a hammock,
the youngest bearer stifling a laugh
as if this were some May Day garden game.
Or at midnight when the winter rain

casts them in black and white,
like a moon-landing on a tiny TV screen,
I huddle in to watch a box fetched
clumsily across a harrowed field.

Such is the magnetism of the dead:
gypsies and suicides, consumptives and virgin brides
the mothers who bled to death in birth
all borne through snows and floods, over bridges,

stepping stones, across running water
the corpse's feet pointing away from home
to baffle the spirit from backtracking.
This is the pedestrian progress of the soul,

a rough-hewn homage and pilgrimage,
travelling sun-wise, in straight lines.
By the spooling river's silver thread,
the corpse-candle of a luminescent owl

carries its cargo of light at ankle height,
pulling silence like a pall over the scene.
And then the track falls quiet again.
No candle burns in the mother church.

No path beneath the crow's black mass.
No coffin-stone to rest the bones.
No witch ball hangs on the rowan tree.
Who'll walk the corpse road back to me?

ENDNOTE

After months of tracing annotations,
crow's feet in the margin's snow,
he is transformed: flesh made word
between the boards. Now pack
his paper life away. Let other
shelves fill with dead men's names.

RING ANGELS

Stunned beside the little copse
at dawn, his maps spread out
across the cooling bonnet:
the ghosts they had sworn
they saw breaking wave on wave
across the radar's blinking baize,

they named them *ring angels*,
like raindrops on a stagnant water table.
These black concentric rings
were starlings leaving their roost.
Across Europe
whole districts were burning.

THE ACT OF FALLING

*'A remarkable picture, showing Anmer, the king's horse, rolling over
jockey Herbert Jones and Emily Davison in the act of falling.'*
Caption accompanying newspaper report, June 1913

I *Flood*

The slender red-head
barricaded in her cell
is a swaying bulrush

as water gushes up
around her knees;
the wardresses gather

by a hose at the door.
She tries to forestall
another force feeding:

a bag of soiled laundry
sent tumbling down
the cast iron staircase,

only to be caught again –
her blood-specked
smock in disarray –

a net slung across
the prison floors,
saving her for this:

terriers at a warren
the wardresses rush in,
her jaw prised open –

a flaccid length
of rubber tube pushed
down her throat,

nursery food, milk and eggs
pumped into the
shrunken acorn of her belly.

II *Post Boxes, &c*

Not the words burned
into the putting green
in the home counties

or the telephone wires
cut by women clothed
for a stroll in the country,

carrying their slack
miles of silence from
Glasgow to London.

Or the orchid house
at Kew, its delicate
exotic freight,

the fruit of Empire's
long embrace, trampled
under kidskin boots.

But the strips of linen,
dipped in paraffin,
laid out like whitefish

each lit rag burning auburn
deposited in postboxes
across the waking capital

where gentlemen
departing for their offices,
stopped to watch letters

to mothers and mistresses
and friends at their club
all lost inside the burning box.

III *Anmer*

His dark flanks
hard as teak
he whinnies,

bares the stained ivory
of his teeth
cribbing and weaving

biting at the boards,
his bandaged tail
a black cosh

slamming
at his rump,
then a sluice of piss

a broken faucet
hissing out across
the unswept concrete

in the nervous,
elongated hour
before the Derby.

IV *Derby Day*

Boaters, top hats,
frock coats, the crowd
swell like a shoal

against the barrier,
pushing the breath
from the chest

of the youngest
among them as
they strain to see

their favourites
round the corner,
the king's colours

blurring somewhere in
the brute grace and
thunder of bloodstock.

No one notices the lady,
pushing courteously
through the crowd

like a governess
who has lost
sight of her child.

V *Impact*

Out on the turf,
the pack bearing down,
she unrolls her flag.

The music hall slapstick
of her attempt to wrap
it about the horse,

then the impact and
its after-image –
the three of them falling –

her skull's muffled crack
a tray of ice broken
open in the Royal Enclosure.

Before her world goes black
she sees her straw hat
blow out along the course,

a bobbing speck
of horse, rider-less
in the middle distance,

its blood pumping a message
from haunch to forelock,
an imperative she understands:

telling it to cross the line
at whatever cost,
to cross the line alone if you must.

CULL

He hangs in the quiet of the cool stone room,
the pendulum in a stopped clock.
His antlers are diviner's rods,
their hazel sways above the pooling blood.
Upwind snows melt, streams quicken,
birds flicker from bough to branch.
His absence has raised the mountain's pulse.

He kept us guessing; we kept low so the wind
would not collude and lead him to suspect us,
carrying the sound of traffic in gridlock, the reek
of burning diesel, litter, children's laughter:
a tincture of the world beyond the heather.
His only natural predator, I closed my eyes
and squeezed the trigger.

PALLBEARERS

No stranger to crematoria
but still shocked so small
a casket could contain you,
your thirty thousand days,
a headland that slips clear
from view: your memories
of oceans, lovers, debtors,
the black cob you clicked
into a trot along a shingle
spit in childhood Norfolk.

My grandmother a frail bird
on the lip of an open cage.
I thought of our last walk
together under the alders,
of the cluster of foxgloves
taken from her garden,
of the Neolithic skeletons
found covered in ochre,
and all that we might mask
with these last, late acts of love
and faith and decoration.